PRESENTED TO:

_____

FROM:

_____

DATE:

_____

ENNEAGRAM TYPE 4

BETH McCORD

Your **Enneagram** Coach

THOMAS NELSON
Since 1798

Enneagram Type 4: The Romantic Individualist

© 2019 by Beth McCord

Published in Nashville, Tennessee, by Thomas Nelson. Thomas Nelson is a registered trademark of HarperCollins Christian Publishing, Inc.

Published in association with Alive Literary Agency.

Unless otherwise noted, Scripture quotations are taken from the ESV® Bible (The Holy Bible, English Standard Version®), copyright © 2001 by Crossway, a publishing ministry of Good News Publishers. Used by permission. All rights reserved.

Any Internet addresses, phone numbers, or company or product information printed in this book are offered as a resource and are not intended in any way to be or to imply an endorsement by Thomas Nelson, nor does Thomas Nelson vouch for the existence, content, or services of these sites, phone numbers, companies, or products beyond the life of this book.

Graphic Designer: Jane Butler, Well Refined Creative Director, wellrefined.co
Interior Designer: Emily Ghattas
Cover Designer: Greg Jackson at Thinkpen Design

ISBN-13: 978-1-4002-1571-3

Printed in China

21 22 23 24 25 GRI 10 9 8 7 6 5 4 3 2

Contents

Foreword

When our twin girls were small, my husband John and I teamed up to take them to the doctor's office for their well-baby checkups. In tiny exam rooms with little more than a board book and some cotton swabs to entertain them, we figured two parents were more likely to keep small children occupied than only one. Eventually the nurse would come in, but no matter how mercifully swift she was, still their faces would wrinkle up in shock when their baby skin was pricked, their eyes reflecting betrayal and disbelief.

But their cries never bothered me in the way they bothered John. While he would tear up, overcome with empathy and sometimes even have to leave the room, I sat quiet with the girls, held them in my lap, knowing their cries would calm down soon enough. Secretly during those doctor visits, I wondered what kind of mother remains unfussed when her children are wailing in pain. *What, in fact, is wrong with me?!*

Years later, the Enneagram gave me language to answer that question. Because not only is there not something wrong with me, but my ability to bear witness to grief and pain without trying to fix it is not a flaw but a gift. I most closely identify with Type 4. Among the many gifts the Enneagram extends, perhaps the greatest one is how, when looked at through the lens of the gospel, it offers us new stories to tell about ourselves, about others, and about God.

I live in a world full of meaning, connection, and possibility, always paying attention to what's going on beneath the surface of things. I value beauty and wonder, and at my best, I have the ability to take an experience and put it into language the soul can understand, process, and apply. But I'm not always at my best. When I forget God's goodness and full acceptance of me, my tendency is to carry a stubborn belief in the false narrative in my head that I'm missing something vital I need for life, that everyone else has that missing piece, and, oh yeah, *they're all in on the joke and I'm the punch line.* My capacity for shame is vast and boundless.

All my life I've carried this question: *Is it possible to belong without blending in?* I long for one and want to avoid the other. But this is a question that keeps me in my false story, and the Enneagram has been an arrow pointing the way out. When circumstances are less than ideal, when all I can see in the world is what's missing, I'm learning to let my disappointment lead me to my center in Christ and to allow Him to reframe what sometimes feels like emptiness into sacred space instead.

When talking about the Enneagram, Fil Anderson, a friend and teacher of mine, said these words I've never forgotten: "It's a wild and wonderful thing to bump into someone and realize it's you." This is the gift of the Enneagram. My weaknesses aren't something I have to try to change, but they can be a starting point for growth. Transformation isn't about changing my personality or becoming someone else, it is about becoming more fully myself as God intended with all the giftedness and nuance of how an Enneagram 4 can reflect the image of God.

And by the way, Type 4s are not as melancholy as the world says we are. It might seem that way from the outside, but what some call sad, we call *normal*. Our ability to sit with sorrow doesn't seem strange or spectacular to us, it just feels like a normal part of the rhythm of our lives, as regular as running errands or as peanut butter and jelly.

If you identify with Type 4 on the Enneagram, I raise my glass to you. Here's to your capacity to hold all that nuance, the shadows and sorrow alongside the light and the joy. Here's to learning more about your unique place among the mystery and beauty of life in the kingdom of God.

Emily P. Freeman, *Wall Street Journal;*
Bestselling Author of *The Next Right Thing*

Introduction

I'm so glad you're here! As an Enneagram teacher and coach, I have seen so many lives changed by the Enneagram. This is a perfect place for you to start your own journey of growth. I'll explain how this interactive book works, but first I'd like to share a little of my story.

Before I learned about the Enneagram, I often unknowingly committed *assumicide*, which is my word for damaging a relationship by assuming I know someone's thoughts, feelings, and motivations. I incorrectly surmise why someone is behaving a particular way and respond (sometimes with disastrous results) without asking clarifying questions to confirm my assumptions or to find out what actually is going on. I've made many wrong and hurtful assumptions about people I dearly love, as well as destructive presumptions about myself.

When my husband, Jeff, and I were in the early years of our marriage, it was a difficult season in our relationship. For the life of me, I couldn't figure out Jeff, or myself. I had been a Christian since I was young and desired to live like Christ, but I kept running into the same stumbling blocks over and over again. I was constantly frustrated, and I longed to understand my heart's motives—*Why do I do what I do?* I figured understanding that might help jolt me out of my rut, but I didn't know where to start.

Then I learned about the insightful tool of the Enneagram, and it was exactly what I needed.

This personality typology (*ennea* for nine; *gram* for diagram) goes beyond what we do (our behaviors) and gets at *why* we do what we do (our heart's motives). And though there are just nine basic personality Types, each Type has multiple layers, allowing for numerous variations of any given personality Type.

The purpose of the Enneagram is to awaken self-awareness and provide hope for growth. Once we learn why each Type thinks, feels, and acts in specific ways, we can look at ourselves with new understanding. Then we can depend on God in new ways to reshape us. The Enneagram makes us aware of when our heart's motives are good and we are on the best path for our personality Type, and when our heart is struggling and veering off course. The Enneagram is an insightful tool, but God's truth is what sets us free and brings transformation.

When I first learned about the Enneagram, I resonated with the Type 9—and had a good laugh when I discovered that 9s know themselves the least! But I finally had wisdom that cleared away the fog and illuminated my inner world. I kept thinking, *Oh, that's why I do that!* Everything started making sense, which brought my restless heart relief.

The Enneagram also helped me see when my heart was aligned with God's truth, misaligned to some degree, or out of alignment entirely with the person God created me to be. It would highlight where I was misunderstanding myself or those I love, and then I could use that awareness to seek transformation. Using the Enneagram from this perspective was a significant turning point for me in all my relationships, especially my marriage. My new perspective allowed me to have more compassion, kindness, forgiveness, mercy, and grace toward others and myself.

Exploring my heart has been some of the hardest—and most rewarding—work I've ever done. The process of looking at our hearts exposes who we are at the core, which highlights our need for redemption and care from God, who is always supplying us with what we need. We simply need to come to Him and depend on Him to change us from the inside out. He will give us a new internal peace, joy, and security that will help us to flourish in new and life-giving ways. The Enneagram can function as an internal GPS, helping you understand why you and others think, feel, and behave in particular ways.

This internal GPS assists you in knowing your current location (your Main Enneagram Type) and your Type's healthiest destination (how your Type can live in alignment with the gospel).

The Enneagram also acts like a rumble strip on the highway—that boundary that makes an irritating sound when your car touches it, warning you when you're about to go off course. It keeps you from swerving into dangerous situations.

While everyone has character traits of all nine Types to varying degrees, we call only one our Main Type. In this book you will unlock some of the mysteries behind *why* you do what you do and discern ways you can grow into your best self.

If you're not sure of your Type number, that's okay! Going through the exercises will help you figure out what your Type number is. Sometimes it's helpful to find out what we're *not* as much as what we are. It's all about self-discovery and self-awareness.

If you find you resonate more with another number, that insight is valuable.

•   •   •

In the twenty-one entries that follow, we'll begin with a summary of your Type. Then we'll discuss topics that are general to the Enneagram and specific to your Type. Each reading will end with reflection questions—prompts to help you write out your thoughts, feelings, and gut reactions to what you have read. Putting pen to paper will help you focus and process what is going on inside you.

Before you begin, I want you to commit to observing your inner world from a nonjudgmental stance. Since God has fully forgiven us, we can observe ourselves without condemnation, guilt, or shame. Instead, we can rest in the fact that we are unconditionally loved, forgiven, and accepted based on what Christ did for us. Follow the prompts and write about your own story. Allow God to transform you from the inside out by helping you see yourself through the lens of the beautiful and amazing Type He designed you to be.

It's my privilege to walk with you as you discover who you are by examining your heart. I'm excited to be on this journey with you!

You are self-aware, self-revealing, and able to communicate about your inner world in ways that inspire others to be true to themselves. You are sensitive, compassionate, and intuitive to others. And you bring a sense of beauty, refinement, and emotional richness into other people's lives.

OVERVIEW OF THE NINE ENNEAGRAM TYPES

The Enneagram (*ennea* = nine, *gram* = diagram) is a map for personal growth that identifies the nine basic ways of relating to and perceiving the world. It accurately describes *why* you think, feel, and behave in particular ways based upon your Core Motivations. Understanding the Enneagram will give you more self-awareness, forgiveness, and compassion for yourself and others.

To find your main Type, take our FREE assessment at test.YourEnneagramCoach.com, and find the Type on the next page that has your Core Motivations—what activates and drives your thoughts, feelings, and behaviors.

Core Motivations of Each Type

 Core Desires: what you're always striving for, believing it will completely fulfill you

 Core Fears: what you're always avoiding and trying to prevent from happening

 Core Weakness: the issue you're always wrestling with, which will remain a struggle until you're in heaven and is a reminder you need God's help on a daily basis

 Core Longing: the message your heart is always longing to hear

Type 1: MORAL PERFECTIONIST

 Core Desire: Having integrity; being good, balanced, accurate, virtuous, and right.

 Core Fear: Being wrong, bad, evil, inappropriate, unredeemable, or corruptible.

 Core Weakness: *Resentment*: Repressing anger that leads to continual frustration and dissatisfaction with yourself, others, and the world for not being perfect.

 Core Longing: You are good.

Type 2: SUPPORTIVE ADVISOR

☀ **Core Desire:** Being appreciated, loved, and wanted.

❗ **Core Fear:** Being rejected and unwanted; being thought worthless, needy, inconsequential, dispensable, or unworthy of love.

❓ **Core Weakness:** *Pride*: Denying your own needs and emotions while using your strong intuition to discover and focus on the emotions and needs of others; confidently inserting your helpful support in hopes that others will say how grateful they are for your thoughtful care.

🔥 **Core Longing:** You are wanted and loved.

Type 3: SUCCESSFUL ACHIEVER

☀ **Core Desire:** Having high status and respect; being admired, successful, and valuable.

❗ **Core Fear:** Being exposed as or thought incompetent, inefficient, or worthless; failing to be or appear successful.

❓ **Core Weakness:** *Deceit*: Deceiving yourself into believing that you are only the image you present to others; embellishing the truth by putting on a polished persona for everyone (including yourself) to see and admire.

🔥 **Core Longing:** You are loved for simply being you.

Type 4: ROMANTIC INDIVIDUALIST

☀ **Core Desire:** Being unique, special, and authentic.

⚠ **Core Fear:** Being inadequate, emotionally cut off, plain, mundane, defective, flawed, or insignificant.

⚗ **Core Weakness:** *Envy*: Feeling that you're tragically flawed, that something foundational is missing inside you, and that others possess qualities you lack.

🔥 **Core Longing:** You are seen and loved for exactly who you are—special and unique.

Type 5: INVESTIGATIVE THINKER

☀ **Core Desire:** Being capable and competent.

⚠ **Core Fear:** Being annihilated, invaded, or not existing; being thought incapable or ignorant; having obligations placed upon you, or your energy being completely depleted.

⚗ **Core Weakness:** *Avarice*: Feeling that you lack inner resources and that too much interaction with others will lead to catastrophic depletion; withholding yourself from contact with the world; holding on to your resources and minimizing your needs.

🔥 **Core Longing:** Your needs are not a problem.

Type 6: LOYAL GUARDIAN

Core Desire: Having security, guidance, and support.

Core Fear: Fearing fear itself; being without support, security, or guidance; being blamed, targeted, alone, or physically abandoned.

Core Weakness: *Anxiety*: Scanning the horizon of life and trying to predict and prevent negative outcomes (especially worst-case scenarios); remaining in a constant state of apprehension and worry.

Core Longing: You are safe and secure.

Type 7: ENTERTAINING OPTIMIST

Core Desire: Being happy, fully satisfied, and content.

Core Fear: Being deprived, trapped in emotional pain, limited, or bored; missing out on something fun.

Core Weakness: *Gluttony*: Feeling a great emptiness inside and having an insatiable desire to "fill yourself up" with experiences and stimulation in hopes of feeling completely satisfied and content.

Core Longing: You will be taken care of.

Type 8: PROTECTIVE CHALLENGER

Core Desire: Protecting yourself and those in your inner circle.

Core Fear: Being weak, powerless, harmed, controlled, vulnerable, manipulated, and left at the mercy of injustice.

Core Weakness: *Lust/Excess*: Constantly desiring intensity, control, and power; willfully pushing yourself on others in order to get what you desire.

Core Longing: You will not be betrayed.

Type 9: PEACEFUL MEDIATOR

Core Desire: Having inner stability and peace of mind.

Core Fear: Being in conflict, tension, or discord; feeling shut out and overlooked; losing connection and relationship with others.

Core Weakness: *Sloth*: Remaining in an unrealistic and idealistic world in order to keep the peace, remain easygoing, and not be disturbed by your anger; falling asleep to your passions, abilities, desires, needs, and worth by merging with others to keep peace and harmony.

Core Longing: Your presence matters.

TYPE 4
KEY MOTIVATIONS

Type 4s are motivated and long to be their most authentic and unique selves. They not only want to feel their emotions but strive to express them in a beautiful and profound way. Their emotions crash in like great tidal waves, which causes them to withdraw so they can take care of their emotional needs before moving forward in other areas of life.

Overview of Type 4

The Romantic Individualist

Authentic | Creative | Expressive
Deep | Temperamental

You bring a distinctive beauty, creativity, and understanding to the world and embrace a wide range of emotions and experiences. In tune with profound despair and suffering, you bravely press into those depths. You are eager to explore our complicated world in search of rich meaning and authentic connection and to look inside yourself to find your unique significance and value.

However, you feel burdened by a sense that you

alone are missing something important. Craving ideal circumstances and love, you often feel disconnected from others or fundamentally flawed. You struggle with feelings of envy as you compare yourself to others, believing they possess the things you long for.

When you forget God's love for you, you can become self-absorbed and temperamental. Painfully self-conscious, you spend a great deal of energy ruminating on how different you are from others, navigating feelings of self-hatred and shame along with emptiness and despair. You may feel anxious around others, always wondering what they think of you, perpetually seeing your weaknesses and never your glory.

Beyond your internal strife, you can get into relational conflicts by being moody, emotionally demanding, withholding, dramatic, and volatile, appearing self-absorbed or disinterested in others.

However, when you bring the longings of your heart to God, you can step away from the waterfall of your emotions and bring forth your gifts in extraordinary ways. You have a strong intuition about others' suffering and can shoulder their deep pains and emotions without being overwhelmed. In fact, it brings you great joy to connect with others on a deep level and to support them in their suffering, which is an amazing gift to the world.

Faith and the Enneagram

Is your heart a mystery to you? Do you need help using the knowledge the Enneagram offers to improve your life? If that's where you are, I'm happy to tell you that there is help and there is hope.

The Bible teaches that God cares about our heart's motives. He "sees not as man sees: man looks on the outward appearance, but the LORD looks on the heart" (1 Samuel 16:7). So we shouldn't look only at our external behaviors; we also need to examine our inner world. For most of us, it's no surprise that the heart of our problem is the problem of our heart!

Before we begin discussing the Enneagram in depth, I'd like to share my beliefs with you for two reasons: First, it's a critical part of how I'll guide you through the Enneagram principles. Second, my faith is what sustains and encourages me, and I believe the same will be true for you.

I believe the Bible is God's truth and the ultimate authority for our lives. Through it, we learn about God's character, love, and wisdom. It brings us close to Him and guides us in the best way to live. My relationship with God brought me healing and purpose before I ever heard of the Enneagram.

Jesus has not been optional for my personal growth; He has been absolutely and utterly vital. He has always come alongside me with love, compassion, and mercy.

I've always wanted my faith to be the most important part of my life, but I spent years frustrated, running into the same issues in my heart over and over again. The Enneagram helped me understand my heart's motives.

As you think about your Type, I'll help you look

at your heart, your life, and your relationships through the lens of the Enneagram. I'll also teach you ways to understand yourself and others and to develop patience and empathy for your differences.

With God working in you and helpful insights from the Enneagram to change awareness and actions, you'll grow into the person you'd like to be more than you've ever dared to dream possible.

When you place your faith in Jesus Christ as your Savior, three life-changing questions are answered, bringing you ultimate grace and freedom:

Am I fully accepted by God (even with all the mess and sin in my life)?

Yes! You are declared righteous. Christ not only purchased forgiveness for your sin but also gave you His perfect righteousness.

Am I loved by God?

Yes! God cherishes you and wants you to be close to Him. He adopted you, making you His beloved child.

Is it really possible for me to change?

Yes! You are being made new. This both *happened* to you and *is happening* to you. This means that you are changed because of what Christ has done, and you are continuing to change as you grow in Christ (it's a bit of a paradox). You can live in an ongoing process of growth by working with the Holy Spirit to become more like Christ, who loves you and gave Himself up for you.

These three life-changing events are what we mean by God's truth, the good news of Christ's finished work on our behalf—"the gospel."

Receiving God's truth and learning about the Enneagram will give you a deeper and richer understanding of *who you are* and *Whose you are*.

When we know *who we are*, we understand our heart's motives and needs and can see God reaching out to meet our needs and giving us grace for our sins through Christ.

And when we know *Whose we are*, we understand that, because of Christ's sacrifice on our behalf, we're God's cherished children. He comforts, sustains, and delights in us. Because of God's character, His love never changes; it doesn't depend on us "getting better" or "doing better" since it hinges solely on what Christ has already done for us. He loves us and desires for us to be in a relationship with Him. We become more like Him by surrendering to Him and depending on the Holy Spirit to transform us.

Which leads us back to looking at who we are. Bringing our faith and the Enneagram together helps us hear God's truths in our mother tongue (kind of like our personality Type's unique language), which enables us to understand God's truth more deeply and will lead to transformation.

Going Deeper

What things have you longed to change about yourself?

_____

_____

_____

_____

_____

_____

_____

_____

_____

How have you attempted to rescue yourself in the past or bring about change on your own? How successful were you?

_____

_____

_____

_____

What difference does knowing you belong to God make in your life?

Being Aware

We can't do anything to make God love us more or love us less since our relationship status has been taken care of solely through Christ's finished work on our behalf. And yet that doesn't mean we're not responsible for participating in our growth. That growth path will look different for different personality Types. We can use the Enneagram to help us find our unique path for transformation as we continue learning and growing. And that's what's super fun about the Enneagram! This insightful tool helps us discover *who we are* and *Whose we are*.

We are not alone on this journey of growth.

God is with us, sustaining us and providing for us. Although we're all uniquely made and no one is alike (it boggles the mind to think about it!), there are commonalities in how we think, feel, and act. The Enneagram shows us nine basic personality Types, each with its own specific patterns of thinking and ways of being: nine *valid* perspectives of the world. Getting to know each of these personality Types increases understanding, compassion, mercy, grace, and forgiveness toward ourselves and others.

Our creative God made us so diverse, yet we all reflect the essence of His character: wise, caring, radiant, creative, knowledgeable, insightful, joyful, protective, and peaceful. As we learn about ourselves and others from the Enneagram, we also learn more about God. Our strengths reflect His attributes.

So how do we begin to find our unique path for growth? By learning about the Enneagram, and by becoming aware of how our heart is doing, which isn't always easy for us. It takes a great deal of time and intentional focus. We start by observing our inner world from a *nonjudgmental* stance. (I don't know how to emphasize this enough!)

Then we can begin to recognize patterns, pause while we are in the present circumstance, and ask ourselves good, clarifying questions about *why* we are thinking, feeling, or behaving in particular ways. We can begin to identify those frustrating patterns we repeat over and over again (the ones we haven't been able to figure out how to stop) and start to think about why we keep doing them.

As I've said before, the Enneagram can act like a rumble strip on a highway, warning you when you're heading off your best path. It lets you know that if you continue in the same direction, drowsy or distracted, you might hurt yourself and others. Alerts about impending danger allow you to course correct, avoid heartache, and experience greater freedom. You will create new patterns of behavior, including a new way of turning to God, when you start to notice the rumble strips in your life.

When you're sensing a rumble strip warning, focus on the acronym AWARE:

- *Awaken*: Notice how you are reacting in your behavior, feelings, thoughts, and body sensations.
- *Welcome*: Be open to what you might learn and observe without condemnation and shame.
- *Ask*: Ask God to help clarify what is happening internally.
- *Receive*: Receive any insight and affirm your true identity as God's beloved child.
- *Enjoy*: Enjoy your new freedom from old self-defeating patterns of living.

Going Deeper

As you look back on your life, when would you have liked a rumble strip to warn you of danger?

_____

_____

_____

_____

_____

_____

In general, what causes you to veer off course and land in a common pitfall (for example, when you're worried)?

_____

_____

_____

_____

_____

_____

SHARING WITH OTHERS
HOW BEST TO LOVE ME

Affirm, appreciate, and encourage
my unique and authentic self.

Tell me of the special and
unique ways I bring significant
value to all areas of life.

Recognize that I have special
abilities in having good intuition.

Please realize that I may not want to
be cheered up when I am melancholy.

Please don't insist that I'm too
sensitive, emotional, or overreacting.

Core Motivations

We'll begin discussing the fundamentals of the Enneagram by looking at our motivations.

Your Core Motivations are the driving force behind your thoughts, feelings, and actions. The internal motivations specific to your Type help explain why you do what you do. (This is why it's impossible to discern someone else's Type. We don't know what motivates them to think, feel, and behave in particular ways. It's their Core Motivations, not their actions, that determine their Type.)

These Core Motivations consist of:

- *Core Fear*: what you're always avoiding and trying to prevent from happening
- *Core Desire*: what you're always striving for, believing it will completely fulfill you
- *Core Weakness*: the issue you're always wrestling with, which will remain a struggle until you're in heaven and is a reminder you need God's help on a daily basis
- *Core Longing*: the message your heart longs to hear

The Enneagram, like a nonjudgmental friend, names and addresses these dynamics of your heart. When you use the Enneagram from a faith-centered approach, you can see how Christ's finished work on your behalf has already satisfied your Core Longing and resolved your Core Fear, Core Desire, and Core Weakness. It's a process to learn how to live in that reality.

When we stray from the truth that we are God's beloved children, it's harder to look inside. After all,

Scripture tells us that "the heart is deceitful . . . and desperately sick" (Jeremiah 17:9). When we forget God's unconditional love for us, we respond to our weaknesses and vulnerabilities with shame or contempt, leaving us feeling worse.

When we only focus on obeying externally, we attempt to look good on the outside but never deal with the source of all our struggles on the inside.

However, when we allow ourselves to rest in the truth that Christ took care of everything for us, we can look at our inner world without fear or condemnation. Real transformation begins when we own our shortcomings.

Here are the Core Motivations of a Type 4:

- *Core Fear*: being inadequate, emotionally cut off, plain, mundane, defective, flawed, or insignificant
- *Core Desire*: being unique, special, and authentic
- *Core Weakness*: envy; feeling that you're tragically flawed, that something

foundational is missing inside you, and that others possess qualities you lack

- *Core Longing*: "You are seen and loved for exactly who you are—special and unique."

The Enneagram exposes the condition of our hearts, and it will tear down any facade we try to hide behind. Since we are God's saved children, we don't have to be afraid of judgment. We can be vulnerable because we know God has taken care of us perfectly through Christ—He has forgiven us and set us free from fear, condemnation, and shame. His presence is a safe place where we can be completely honest about where we are. With this freedom, allow the Enneagram to be a flashlight to your heart's condition. Let it reveal how you are doing at any given moment so you can remain on the best path for your personality Type.

Going Deeper

How challenging is it for you to look at the condition of your heart?

_____

_____

_____

_____

_____

_____

What response do you typically have when you recognize your struggles?

_____

_____

_____

_____

_____

_____

How would you like to respond when the struggles inside you are exposed?

_____

_____

_____

_____

_____

_____

_____

_____

_____

_____

_____

_____

_____

_____

_____

_____

_____

Core Fear

Understanding your Core Fear is the first step in identifying your motivations. Your personality believes it's vital to your well-being that you constantly spend time and energy avoiding this thing you fear. It is the lens through which you see the world, the "reality" you believe. You assume others do, or should, see the world through this lens, and you may become confused and dismayed when they don't.

Your Core Fear as a Type 4 is being inadequate, emotionally cut off, plain, mundane, defective, flawed, or insignificant.

You don't want to be ordinary, normal, or

restricted in expressing your most authentic self throughout all facets of life. You don't want your individual tastes, creativity, or aesthetics to be questioned, and you'd rather not be with those who don't appreciate emotional depth and beauty.

Even though you fear being plain, flawed, or inadequate, here's what is true: God created you exactly the way He desires you to be—unique and special.

He made no mistakes in designing you. He created you to experience deep emotions and love beauty and connection. He wants you to express your creativity, just as He has. He made you to stand out and bless others with your unique expression of yourself and your perspective on the world.

When your Core Fears get activated, use them as a rumble strip to alert you. Then pause, become AWARE, and reorient yourself with what is true so your heart can rest in His passion for you.

MY CORE FEARS

TYPE 4
THE ROMANTIC
INDIVIDUALIST

Being inadequate, emotionally cut off, plain, mundane, defective, flawed, or insignificant

Going Deeper

What comes to mind when you think about your Core Fear?

_____

_____

_____

_____

_____

_____

_____

_____

_____

_____

_____

_____

_____

_____

_____

_____

_____

Do any particular words in the Type 4 Core Fear description ring true for you?

_____

_____

_____

_____

_____

_____

_____

_____

_____

_____

_____

_____

_____

_____

_____

What strategies have you used in the past to protect yourself from your fears?

Core Desire

Understanding your Core Desire is the next step in identifying your motivations. Your Core Desire is what you're always striving for, believing it will ultimately fulfill you.

While your personality Type is running away from your Core Fear, it's also running toward your Core Desire. You believe that once you have this Core Desire met, all of life will be okay and you will feel fully satisfied and content. This longing to experience your Core Desire constantly propels you to focus your efforts on pursuing and obtaining it.

As a Type 4, you desire to be unique and special and to authentically express yourself in something beautiful. You want to connect with others on a deep and meaningful level and to care for your emotions before moving forward with anything else.

God knows your Core Desire, and He freely gives it to you. He knows you intimately, seeing how truly special and beautiful you are. He pursues you and delights in you, recognizing that there is no one quite like you. He understands all of your deep emotions and can meet you in those depths. As you draw nearer to Him, He will bring meaning to every aspect of your life and continually remind you of His presence and enduring love.

Not everyone has the same Core Desire as you. Take time to recognize that others are just as passionate in obtaining their Core Desire as you are in gaining yours. This awareness will help you navigate relationship dynamics, enabling you to offer more empathy, compassion, and grace. Use the Enneagram to know yourself better so you can better communicate with others about what is happening inside your heart. Then be curious about others, and ask them to reveal to you *their* desires so you can get to know them on a deeper level.

MY CORE DESIRES

TYPE 4
THE ROMANTIC
INDIVIDUALIST

Being unique, special, and authentic

Going Deeper

As you look back over your life, what aspects of the Type 4 Core Desire have you been chasing?

_____

_____

_____

_____

_____

_____

_____

_____

Describe ways you have attempted to pursue these specific desires.

_____

_____

_____

_____

What would it feel like to trust in the fact that God has already met your Core Desire?

Core Weakness

Deep inside, you struggle with a Core Weakness, which is your Achilles' heel. This one issue repeatedly causes you to stumble in life. At times you might find some relief. But as hard as you try to improve on your own, your struggle in this area continually resurfaces.

God's encouraging words to you are that when you are weak, He is strong. This brings hope that you are not destined to be utterly stuck in your weakness. As you grow closer to God and depend on Him, He will lessen the constraint your Core Weakness has over you and help you move out of your rut.

As a Type 4, your Core Weakness is *envy*. You

feel that you're tragically flawed, that something foundational is missing inside you, and that others possess the qualities you lack.

Imagine that everyone has a puzzle that represents them. You feel everyone's puzzle is neatly put together and complete, and yours is not. You feel your puzzle has a big missing piece, making it defective and flawed. You envy others, believing they have what you lack. This creates a deep longing within you to find something special and different about yourself so that others will look past your flaws and see your creativity, beauty, and depth.

Fueled by a constant need to search deep within to find your authentic self and display it for others, you fear anything that might hinder this effort. You constantly feel misunderstood.

God made you, and He never makes a mistake. He delights in what He created and desires for you to become your most authentic self, which is a beautiful reflection of Him.

By shifting your focus to who you already are in God's eyes, you can rest knowing that you were created to be unique and beautiful, and that you are fully known, understood, and cherished. You will no longer need to be different and stand out to receive others' love for you because you have God's full love and acceptance.

When you see your Core Weakness surfacing, think of it as a rumble strip, alerting you that you can easily veer off course into your common pitfalls of envying what others have since you believe you are tragically flawed and defective, and therefore feel shame. Use this awareness to "recalculate" your inner world so you can get back to your healthiest path.

Going Deeper

What comes to mind as you think about your Core Weakness?

_____

_____

_____

_____

In what ways have you wrestled with envy throughout your life?

_____

_____

_____

_____

_____

_____

_____

What specific things are you facing now that your Core Weakness impacts?

_____

_____

_____

_____

_____

_____

_____

MY CORE WEAKNESS

TYPE 4
THE ROMANTIC
INDIVIDUALIST

Envy — feeling that you're tragically flawed, that something foundational is missing inside you, and that others possess the qualities you lack

Core Longing

Your Core Longing is the message your heart is always yearning to receive, what you've craved since you were a child. Throughout life, you've been striving to hear this message from your family members, friends, teachers, coaches, and bosses. No matter how much you've tried to get others to communicate this message to you, you've never felt it was delivered to the degree your heart needed it.

As a Type 4, your Core Longing is to hear, "You are seen and loved for exactly who you are—special and unique."

You have believed that if you could be authentic, different, and unique enough, then others would communicate this message to you, whether in verbal or nonverbal ways. However, even those who have tried their best to do this for you are unable to satisfy this longing that runs so deep inside you.

Why? Because people *cannot* give you all you need. Only God can. When you're trying to receive this message apart from God, you will always thirst for more. But when you listen to Him and see that He's drawing you to Himself, then you will find fulfillment and freedom.

How does God meet your Core Longing?

1. **He sees you.**

   God sees not only all your unique abilities that reflect Him but also your sorrows and needs. He sent Jesus to rescue you from brokenness and bring you close to Him. He delights in seeing you and coming to your rescue with His great love.

2. **He understands you.**

   You feel misunderstood and different, but God completely understands, loves, and cherishes you—who you really are. God created you to be unique, and He delights in His creation. Knowing this, you can fully rest in the truth that you are seen and loved for exactly who you are.

When you feel defective and misunderstood, use the Enneagram as the rumble strip to alert you of what is true: that you are cherished and known by God. Allow it to point out how you are believing false messages so you can live your life more grounded in His truth rather than false emotional fantasies.

Going Deeper

How have you seen your Core Longing at work in your life?

_____

_____

_____

_____

What did that look like when you were a child?

_____

_____

_____

_____

_____

_____

_____

_____

_____

_____

_____

_____

How does it appear in your life as an adult?

_____

_____

_____

_____

_____

_____

_____

_____

_____

_____

_____

_____

Describe how you feel and what you think when you read that God answers your longing.

_____

_____

_____

_____

_____

_____

_____

MY CORE LONGING

**TYPE 4
THE ROMANTIC
INDIVIDUALIST**

The message my heart always longs to hear.

"You are seen and loved for exactly
who you are—special and unique."

Directional Signals of the Enneagram

Just as a GPS gives directional signals such as "Approaching right turn" or "Proceed to the high-lighted route," the Enneagram guides us in which way to go. But we still need to pay attention to where we're heading and reroute our course when necessary.

The Enneagram provides directions in a couple of ways: (1) by pointing out how aligned with God's truth we are, and (2) by showing us what other Types we are connected to and how we might take on those Types' characteristics in different life situations. We do not *become* the Types we are

YOUR INTERNAL GPS

It reveals **why** you think, feel, and behave in particular ways, so you can steer your internal life in the best direction for your personality Type.

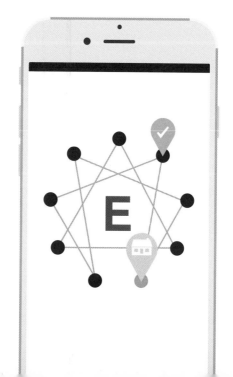

connected to; we remain our Main Type (with its Core Fear, Desire, Weakness, and Longing) as we access the other Types' attributes.

The directional signals of the Enneagram make us aware of which way our heart is heading and where we might end up. Whether it's a good or bad direction depends on various factors—it can change day by day as we take on positive or negative qualities of other Types.

When we are headed in the wrong direction, the steps to turning around and getting back on track are simply owning our mistakes, turning from them, asking for forgiveness from God and others, and asking God to restore us to the best path.

The directional signals we'll discuss in the following entries are: the Levels of Alignment with God's Truth, the Wings, the Triads, and the Enneagram Paths. Hang in there! I'll guide you through these signals, which will help you discover who you are and Whose you are, and show you the healthiest path for your personality Type.

Type 4

HOW I TYPICALLY COMMUNICATE

When I am doing well, I am authentic, deep, empathetic, a great listener when others are sad or grieving, and I express my emotions with inner balance.

When I am not doing well, I can be moody, emotionally intense and explosive, cold and detached, condescending, and steer the conversation to focus on me.

Levels of Alignment with God's Truth

The first set of directional signals we'll discuss are the Levels of Alignment with God's truth. The inspiration for these levels comes from the apostle Paul, who wrote in Galatians 2:14 that some of the early Christian leaders' conduct was not in step (aligned) with God's truth. To grow in our particular personality Type, we must be in step with God's truth and design for us.

We all move fluidly through the Levels of Alignment from day to day. The level at which we find ourselves at any given moment depends on our heart's condition and how we're navigating through life.

Healthy	**Aligned with God's Truth** (Living as His Beloved)
Average (Autopilot)	**Misaligned with God's Truth** (Living in Our Own Strength)
Unhealthy	**Out of Alignment with God's Truth** (Living as an Orphan)

When we are resting, believing, and trusting in who we are in Christ, we are living as His beloved (healthy and aligned with God's truth). We are no longer using our personality strategies to meet our needs and desires. Instead, we are coming to our God, who we know loves us and will provide for us.

When our heart and mind begin to wander from that truth, we start to believe that we must take some control and live in our own strength, even though He is good and sovereign (average/auto-pilot level).

Then there are times when we completely forget that we are His beloved children. In this state of mind, we think we're all alone, that we're orphans who have to handle all of life on our own (unhealthy level).

But no matter where we are on the Levels of Alignment, we are always His cherished children. Christ's life, death, and resurrection accomplished everything required for us to be His. Therefore, no matter what state our heart is in, we can *rejoice* in His work in our lives, *repent* if we need to, and fully *rest* in who we are in Him.

As you can imagine, a group of people with the same personality Type (same Core Fear, Desire, Weakness, and Longing) can look vastly different from each other due to varying alignments with God's truth.

In the readings that follow, we will consider how you as a Type 4 function at the three Levels of Alignment.

Going Deeper

At what Level of Alignment do you think your heart is at the moment?

_____

_____

_____

_____

_____

_____

_____

_____

_____

_____

In what season of life have you thrived the most, not feeling limited by your fears and weaknesses?

_____

_____

_____

_____

_____

_____

_____

_____

_____

_____

_____

What do you think contributed to that growth?

_____

_____

_____

_____

_____

_____

_____

_____

_____

_____

_____

When You Are Aligned

When the condition of your heart is healthy, you align with God's truth that you are fully taken care of by Christ.

As a Type 4 at this level, you are creative, emotionally honest, connected, and inspired by beauty. You trust that you are already God's special and beloved child; therefore, you do not need to strive to be unique to receive unconditional love. You realize God sees and understands you 100 percent of the time and that He loves you for exactly who you are. You see your significance through His eyes.

Because you now believe that you are not defective or flawed, you stop comparing yourself to others and let go of envy. You rest knowing you lack nothing and have all you need. Sensitive and intuitive both to others and yourself, you are gentle, tactful, and compassionate.

Recognizing that you are uniquely made for God and that He treasures you, you can freely be yourself without fear. You are highly individualistic, true to yourself, and emotionally honest. You can be simultaneously serious and funny, vulnerable and strong.

Going Deeper

When are you at your best and most trusting of God?

_____

_____

_____

_____

_____

_____

What differences do you notice in your thinking and in your life when you're in that state?

_____

_____

_____

_____

_____

_____

_____

What helps you stay in alignment with God's plan for your personality Type?

_____

_____

_____

_____

_____

_____

_____

Write about a time when you've exhibited emotional balance, deep compassion for others, or any other indicators of healthy alignment.

When You Are Misaligned

Even though we know God is good and in control, there are times when our hearts and minds wander away from the truth that God loves us and has fully provided for us in the finished work of Christ on our behalf. In this average or autopilot level of health, we start to believe that we must take some control and live in our own strength.

As a Type 4 at this level, your sense of reality starts to come from your passionate feelings and imagination. You take an artistic, romantic orientation to life, creating a beautiful, aesthetic environment to cultivate and prolong your feelings.

Relying on your emotions too much, you internalize your experiences and take every disappointment personally. You can become self-absorbed, moody, hypersensitive, and self-conscious. You might withdraw from others to protect your self-image and sort out your feelings.

You begin to think you are different from others and exempt from living as everyone else does. Focusing on your feelings not only drives you deeper into a melancholic state but also gives them more power—soon your emotions alone inform your view of reality and truth.

Listening to others becomes difficult since you always feel misunderstood. Self-pity and envy lead you to more self-indulgence and an increasingly impractical and unproductive state of life.

MY HIDDEN STRUGGLE

TYPE 4

The unending yearning to be a
particular kind of person, someone
who is uniquely talented, socially
adept, and intensely desired

The nagging longing to be somehow
different from who I am in order to be
seen and loved, constantly comparing
myself with others and the ideal version
of myself I've created in my mind

The inability to see and
appreciate the unique and
positive attributes of who I am

Going Deeper

What aspects of your behavior and life indicate that you are becoming misaligned?

_____

_____

_____

In what ways do you attempt to live in your own strength, not in your identity as a person God loves?

_____

_____

_____

What can you do when you begin to catch yourself in misalignment?

_____

_____

_____

When You Are Out of Alignment Entirely

When we completely forget that our status never changes and we are still His beloved based on what Christ did for us, we think and believe we're all alone, like an orphan.

Problems begin to multiply when you need others to appreciate your uniqueness and emotional depth in the same way you do. When you see that they do not understand your original style, you can spiral downward. You feel misunderstood, defective, flawed, and alone. These feelings cause even more sadness. Overcome with these intense emotions, you become self-absorbed, temperamental, and moody, feeling you're missing something vital inside.

You may manipulate others by creating emotional drama and acting like you are the victim, hoping that someone will be inclined to "rescue" you. Unfortunately, this tactic usually pushes people away. When this happens, you can feel a great deal of shame and fall into depression, since you are constantly focusing on your emotions. You may feel paralyzed until you can sort out your feelings.

This cycle will continue until you realize that God is a loving and caring Father to you. When you begin to believe this truth and depend on Him completely, you will move up the levels of health.

Going Deeper

In what seasons of life have you been most out of alignment with God's truth?

_____

_____

_____

_____

_____

_____

What does this level look like for you (specific behaviors, beliefs, etc.)?

_____

_____

_____

_____

_____

_____

Who in your life can best support and encourage you when you're struggling and guide you back to health?

The Wings

The next set of directional signals we'll discuss are the Wings, which are the two numbers *directly* next to your Main Type's number on the Enneagram diagram. As I've said, we access the characteristics of the Type on either side of us while remaining our Main Type. So everyone's Enneagram personality is a combination of one Main Type and the two Types adjacent to it.

As a Type 4, your Wings are 3 and 5. You'll often see it written this way: 4w3 or 4w5.

Everyone uses their Wings to varying degrees and differently in different circumstances, but it's common for a person to rely more on one Wing than another.

You can think of the Wings like salt and pepper. Each Wing adds a unique "flavor" to your personality, bringing complexity to your Main Type. Just as a delicious filet mignon doesn't *become* the salt or pepper we season it with, we don't become our Wings. Our Wings influence our Main Type in varying ways, both positively and negatively, depending on where we are on the Levels of Alignment. We know that too much salt or pepper can make that filet inedible, but the right balance can enhance our enjoyment of it significantly.

When we align with God's truth, we can access the healthy aspects of our Wings. When we are misaligned or out of alignment with God's truth, we will often draw from the average or unhealthy aspects of our Wings. And like under seasoning or over seasoning our perfectly cooked steaks, it can make a huge difference.

Learning how to use our Wings correctly can dramatically alter our life experiences. Applying "seasoning"—utilizing the healthy attributes of our Wings—can help us change course. As we return to believing and trusting in God, we can express ourselves more fully and be seen for who we really are.

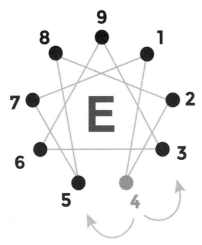

Type 4 with Wing 3 (4w3), The Aristocrat: This combination can be emotionally vivid and buoyant. Type 3 is more extroverted, upbeat, goal-oriented, and interpersonal, which can keep Type 4 from being withdrawn, quiet, and introverted. Both are especially concerned about image and self-esteem. Type 4 desires to be authentic to one's true self, but Type 3 needs accomplishments to be validated.

If you're an Aristocrat, you see yourself as having a more refined taste than others. You focus on leaving your mark on the world through creative accomplishments.

When you are struggling, you begin to be more consumed with what others think of you, envy what others have, and instigate heightened emotional drama.

Type 4 with Wing 5 (4w5), The Bohemian: Both of these types withdraw from others. Type 4 protects emotions, while Type 5 protects inner resources.

If you're a Bohemian, you are more introverted and isolated than the Aristocrat. You may have more intellectual depth and originality. Remarkably creative, unusual, and mysterious, you combine intelligence with emotional intuition to produce stunning original works. Bohemians are less ambitious or concerned with what others think.

When you are struggling, your emotional and intellectual world takes over and becomes your reality, causing you to accomplish less. You may withdraw and become fiercely independent.

 **WINGS**

Type 4 with 3 Wing (4w3)
"The Aristocrat"
They are more extroverted, competitive, upbeat, ambitious, emotionally volatile, concerned with image, and flamboyant.

Type 4 with 5 Wing (4w5)
"The Bohemian"
They are more introverted, intellectual, withdrawn, reserved, observant, eccentric, depressed, and have intellectual depth.

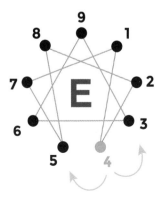

Going Deeper

Which Wing do you use more?

_____

_____

_____

_____

_____

_____

_____

How have you seen this Wing enhance your Main Type?

_____

_____

_____

_____

_____

_____

How does it impact your relationships, work, and everyday life?

_____

_____

_____

_____

_____

_____

_____

_____

_____

_____

_____

_____

_____

_____

_____

_____

How does the other Wing influence your Main Type?

_____

_____

_____

_____

_____

_____

_____

_____

_____

How can you utilize it more to create balance?

_____

_____

_____

_____

_____

_____

_____

_____

_____

The Triads

The next set of directional signals we'll discuss are the Triads. We can group the nine personality Types in many ways, and the most common one is by group-ings of three, or Triads. The three Types in each group share common assets and liabilities. For each person one Triad is more dominant (the one with your Main Type) than the other two.

Though we could name several different Triads within the Enneagram, the best known is the Center of Intelligence Triad:

- Feeling Center (Heart Triad): Types 2, 3, and 4
- Thinking Center (Head Triad): Types 5, 6, and 7
- Instinctive Center (Gut Triad): Types 8, 9, and 1

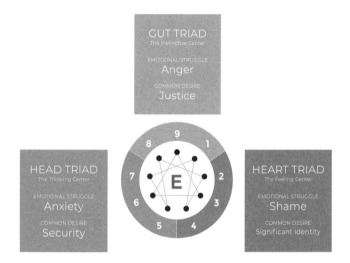

Two commonalities drive the Enneagram Types in each of these three centers: a common emotional imbalance and a common desire.

In the Heart Triad, Types 2, 3, and 4 are imbalanced in their *feelings*. This group shares similar assets and liabilities related to how they feel and engage in life through their feelings. Type 2s feel other people's emotions. Type 3s access their emotions the least, concerned that those emotions will hinder them from accomplishing goals and tasks.

Type 4s feel all their emotions with depth and intensity. All three Types react to their *emotional struggles* with *shame*.

Those in the Heart Triad focus on a desire for a *specific identity or significance* that they want others to see and recognize. Type 2s want to be seen as the most supportive, caring, and selfless person. Type 3s want to be seen as the most successful, admirable, and accomplished person. And Type 4s want to be seen as special, different, and unique.

When you are healthy as a Type 4, you are very self-aware and self-revealing, able to communicate about your inner world in a way that helps others do the same.

However, when you are struggling, you try to maintain a self-image of being completely different from everyone else and feel misunderstood. You begin to believe that your emotions are reality and start to trust your imaginings of what others feel about you.

Sadness, melancholy, and longing are all part of your emotional struggle with shame. You do not

ENNEAGRAM TYPE 4

At Their Best	At Their Worst
Authentic	Withdrawn
Warm	Exaggerated Moods
Compassionate	Depressed
Introspective	Self-Pitying
Expressive	Moralistic
Creative	Self-Absorbed
Supportive	Stubborn
Refined	Possessive
Unique	Temperamental

want others to force you to put your feelings and self-image aside until you have fully worked through the depths of your emotions. You can become depressed and withdrawn from others when feelings of shame and self-hatred spin out of control.

Going Deeper

What stands out to you about being in the Feeling Triad and your propensity for feelings of shame?

_____

_____

_____

_____

_____

_____

_____

_____

_____

How attuned are you to your thinking and gut instincts in comparison to feelings?

_____

_____

_____

_____

_____

_____

_____

In what ways do you wrestle with shame and feel the need to express your authentic self?

_____

_____

_____

_____

_____

_____

_____

Do your efforts bring the acceptance and love and deep longings you want?

_____

_____

_____

_____

_____

_____

Where do your strengths of self-awareness, authenticity, and creativity shine the most?

_____

_____

_____

_____

_____

_____

Childhood Message

Before we discuss the last set of directional signals (the Enneagram Paths), we need to understand what the Enneagram calls a Childhood Message.

From birth, everyone has a unique perspective on life, our personality Type's perspective. We all tend toward particular assumptions or concerns, and these develop into a Childhood Message. Our parents, teachers, and authority figures may have directly communicated this message to us, but most of the time, we interpreted what they said or did through the lens of our personality Type to fit this belief.

Sometimes we can see a direct correlation

between our Childhood Message and a childhood event; other times we can't. Somewhere, somehow, we picked up a message that rang true for us because of our personality Type's hardwiring. This false interpretation of our circumstances was and still is painful to us, profoundly impacting us as children and as adults.

Gaining insight into how our personality Type interpreted events and relationships in childhood will help us identify how that interpretation is impacting us today. Believing our Childhood Message causes our personality to reinforce its strategies to protect us from our Core Fear—apart from God's truth. Once we understand that the message is hardwired into our thinking, we can experience God's healing truth and live more freely.

What's more, when we know the Childhood Message of others, we can begin to understand why they do what they do and how we can communicate with them more effectively.

As a Type 4, your Childhood Message is: "It is not okay to be too much or not enough."

The message your heart longed to hear as a child is your Core Longing: "You are seen and loved for exactly who you are—special and unique."

•   •   •

Type 4 children often felt different from and misunderstood by their parents, siblings, and others. Not seeing themselves reflected in their parents led to feelings of disconnection, abandonment, and loneliness.

They perceived their parents as not taking a deep interest in knowing them completely or even trying to understand how unique and special they were. This led them to feel rejected, like there was something fundamentally missing and flawed about them.

Since they could not see themselves in their parents, they turned inward to find their authentic selves. Discovering and understanding the depths of themselves became their most important goal, believing it would bring them self-esteem.

Unfortunately, the more they explored their

internal selves, the more dissatisfied they became because they never found their "missing piece." This cycle created a vortex. The more they felt misunderstood, rejected, and ashamed, the deeper they dove within. When they still did not find the satisfaction they were longing for, they sank even deeper. They became extremely self-focused, self-absorbed, moody, and temperamental.

These children put much effort into showing others their uniqueness and special identity, hoping to receive affirmation. They were looking for someone who would deeply love and cherish them for just being their authentic selves.

Knowing your personality Type's Childhood Message will help you break free from childhood perceptions and reinterpret pieces of your story from a better vantage point. As you explore this, be gracious to yourself and your past. Be sensitive, nonjudgmental, caring, and kind to yourself. And remember, only God can fully redeem your past. He can free you from chains that bind, heal wounds that linger, and restore you to freedom.

Going Deeper

*To what degree do you relate to the Type 4
Childhood Message?*

_____

_____

_____

_____

_____

_____

_____

What stories come to mind when you hear it?

_____

_____

_____

_____

_____

_____

_____

What circumstances in the present have repeated
this message from the past?

_____

_____

_____

_____

_____

_____

_____

What advice would you give to your childhood self
in light of this message?

_____

_____

_____

_____

_____

_____

_____

_____

Enneagram Paths

The final directional signals we'll discuss are the Enneagram Paths, which the inner lines and arrows in the Enneagram diagram display. The lines and arrows going out from our Main Type point to our Connecting Types. As a Type 4, you connect to Types 2 and 1.

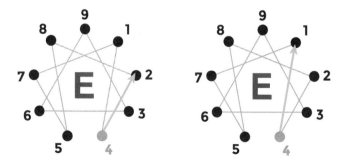

Remember, we can access both positive and negative characteristics of a Type we are connected to. The kind we access depends on whether we are aligned, misaligned, or out of alignment with God's truth.

Here is an overview of the four Enneagram Paths, which we'll discuss further in the following readings:

- *Stress Path*: When we're under stress, we tend to take on some of the misaligned or out-of-alignment characteristics of our Stress Path Type. For Type 4, these are the negative aspects of Type 2.
- *Blind Spot Path*: When we're around those we're most familiar with (mainly family), we display the misaligned characteristics of our Blind Spot Path Type. We typically do not see these characteristics in ourselves easily. For Type 4, these are the negative aspects of Type 1.
- *Growth Path*: When we believe and trust

that God loves us and that all He has is ours in Christ, we begin to move in a healthier direction, accessing the aligned characteristics of our Connecting Type. For Type 4, these are the positive aspects of Type 1.

- *Converging Path*: After making progress on the Growth path, we can reach the most aligned point of our Type, which is where three healthy Types come together. Here we access the healthiest qualities of our Main Type, our Growth Path's Type, and our Stress Path's Type.

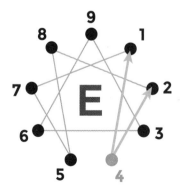

Going Deeper

In what direction is your heart currently heading?

_____

_____

_____

_____

_____

_____

_____

What concerns are you wrestling with?

_____

_____

_____

_____

_____

_____

_____

What growth have you experienced recently?

_____

_____

_____

_____

_____

_____

_____

When you look at the four paths, what path have you been traveling recently? Why?

_____

_____

_____

_____

_____

_____

_____

Stress Path

Under stress, you tend to move in the direction of the arrow below, taking on some of the misaligned characteristics of Type 2. Learning to identify these behavior patterns can serve as a rumble strip warning that you're veering off course. Then you can

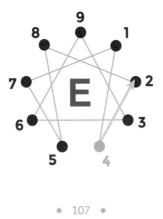

stop, pray for God's help, and move in a healthier direction for your personality.

As a Type 4 moving toward the average or unhealthy Type 2, you may:

- defend your hurt feelings by withdrawing or removing your attention and affection.
- become over-involved and clingy to win affection.
- discuss the current condition of your relationships with others so they'll see their need for you.
- manipulate and create dependency through helping, giving attention, and doing favors for others.
- become possessive and constantly want to be close and secure in relationships.
- use flattery to gain attention from others when feeling empty or lonely.

Going Deeper

Describe a stressful time when you took on some of these tendencies. What was the situation, and why were you triggered to respond this way?

When have you used clingy or manipulative behaviors to cope with stress and feeling overwhelmed?

_____

_____

_____

_____

_____

_____

What tendencies do you notice about yourself in times of stress?

_____

_____

_____

_____

_____

_____

_____

What things in your life cause the most stress for you?

TYPE 4 UNDER STRESS

When under stress, **Type 4** will start to exhibit some of the average to unhealthy characteristics of **Type 2**.

Becoming over-involved and clingy

Trying to manipulate others into loving them

Doing favors and reminding others of how they have supported them

DAY 18

Blind Spot Path

When you're around people you're most familiar with—family members or close friends—you
express yourself more freely. You show them parts
of yourself you don't show anyone else, for better
or worse. When you're uninhibited and not at your
best, you display the negative qualities of your personality. On this Blind Spot Path, you access the
misaligned attributes of your Connecting Type,
which is Type 1.

You may be unaware that you're behaving differently with your family members or close friends
than you are with other people. Be sure to take
note of this path when you're trying to understand

yourself and your reactions, because it may surprise you. Working on these negative aspects can
improve the relationship dynamics with those you're
closest to.

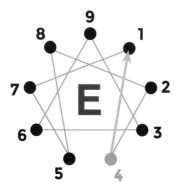

As a Type 4 moving toward the average or
unhealthy Type 1, you may:

- focus on flaws, becoming more judgmental
  and critical of others.
- be vocal about what you see as wrong.
- visibly display your displeasure and
  disappointment.

- become impatient, picky, and controlling, constantly annoyed and irritated with flaws and imperfections you see.
- try to address inadequacies in others through sharing dissatisfaction and disappointment.
- criticize yourself for personal imperfections that leap out at you.

Going Deeper

How do you respond when you feel overwhelmed in the presence of people you feel secure with versus those you're less comfortable with?

Which of the average or unhealthy tendencies do you resonate with the most?

_____

_____

_____

_____

_____

_____

_____

_____

Describe a situation where you reacted in the ways described above.

_____

_____

_____

_____

_____

_____

_____

_____

Growth Path

When you believe and trust that God loves you, and all He has is yours, you begin to relax and let go of your personality's constraints and lies. You draw nearer to Him and move in a direction that aligns you with His truth. You feel safe, secure, and loved.

Feeling more joy, peace, and liberation, you stretch yourself toward healthier attributes, even though it is hard. As you grow in faith and depend solely on Him, God blesses you with real and lasting transformation, shaping you into who He made you to be.

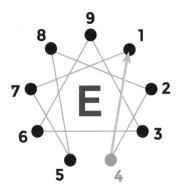

As a Type 4 moving toward the healthy side of Type 1, you may:

- become more emotionally balanced, objective, and principled.
- embrace mundane tasks as opportunities to be a good steward and to be responsible and organized.
- become focused, disciplined, and grounded.
- be productive and do what is right.
- complete what needs to be addressed before moving onto other interests.

Going Deeper

When you are growing, what changes about your heart and your typical responses?

_____

_____

_____

_____

_____

_____

Which of these growth attributes would you love to experience more in your life?

_____

_____

_____

_____

_____

_____

What helps to support your growth and flourishing?

How can you incorporate those things into your life more?

TYPE 4 DIRECTION OF GROWTH

When moving in the direction of growth, **Type 4** will start to exhibit some of the healthier characteristics of **Type 1**.

Becoming more objective and principled

Becoming more present in the here and now; not allowing their emotions to control them

Becoming more practical, self-disciplined, and grounded

Converging Path

You are your best self on the Converging Path, where three Types come together. Here you access the healthiest qualities of your Main Type, your Growth Path's Type, and your Stress Path's Type. When you live in the fullness of who you really are in Christ, you are freed from the bonds of your personality.

This path of personal transformation can be difficult to reach and maintain. When you first learn about the Converging Path, you may feel it's too hard to travel. But God wants to provide this path for you. Trust Him, follow Him, and ask Him to be with you as you move forward.

As a Type 4 moving toward the healthy side of Type 2, you can:

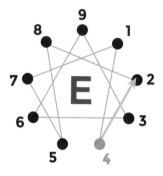

- know your value and love yourself unconditionally.
- put the needs of others ahead of your own.
- see what you possess and express gratitude, instead of longing for what is missing.
- acknowledge positive qualities in others and openly affirm them.
- selflessly support and care for others without needing attention.
- experience others' emotions and needs.

Going Deeper

Can you recall a time when you experienced the freedom and joy of the Converging Path?

_____

_____

_____

_____

_____

_____

What was it like when you accessed the healthiest aspects of your Main Type, Growth Path's Type, and Stress Path's Type?

_____

_____

_____

_____

_____

_____

What would help you move toward your Converging Path more often?

Spiritual Renewal **TYPE 4 THE ROMANTIC INDIVIDUALIST**

GOING DEEPER

Grab a journal and make a list of everything you're thankful for. Reflect on all the ways God has blessed your life and all the gifts you've been given. Ask God to remind you that nothing is missing and that He's given you everything you need to be content.

Moving Toward Your Best Self

The journey of exploring your heart is not an easy one, but it's an exciting one.

God has a unique message for each Type. The message He tells you as a Type 4 is: "You are seen and loved for who you truly are. You are special and unique."

He has given you the most significant identity as His wonderful creation and His beloved child. He rescued you from loneliness, sorrow, grief, and the need for attention from others to prove how unique you are.

Every Enneagram Type experiences brokenness and needs to be rescued. Every Type is missing a vital piece, and that piece is Christ. Knowing that others struggle and also need a Rescuer helps you move toward them with compassion and connection, focusing less on yourself.

You are not alone. You are part of a bigger story, a beautiful tapestry that God is weaving together. Your life is a unique thread that is being woven into this tapestry. You bring deep meaning to life and your community with your creativity and eye for beauty. Without your gifts, God's tapestry would not be as vibrant. He desired creativity and beauty, so He created you to bring it about in the world.

Each Type has a signature Virtue, which you exhibit when you are at your best, and Type 4s Virtue is *equanimity (emotional balance)*.

At your best, you are creative, emotionally honest, connected, and inspired by beauty. You see that you are not defective or flawed, which frees you to let go of envy. You understand you are not lacking anything and find all you long for in God's deep love for you, which allows you to have more emotional balance.

Secure in His love, you can rest knowing that He will never leave you or forsake you. This brings great comfort and eases your heart, so you're able to move forward in relationships, even when a relationship is in a difficult stage. You can focus on others and care for them on a deep level. Others feel your empathy and compassion, which brings them deep healing.

Using the Enneagram from a biblical perspective can empower you to see yourself with astonishing clarity so you can break free from self-condemnation, fear, and shame by experiencing unconditional love, forgiveness, and freedom. In Him, you are whole. And with Him by your side, you can grow stronger and healthier every day.

Now that you know how to use this internal GPS and its navigational signals, start using it every day. Tune in to how your heart is doing. Avoid your common pitfalls by staying alert to your rumble strips. As you learn new awareness and actions, you will move forward on the path that is healthiest for your personality Type and experience the gift of tremendous personal growth.

Going Deeper

What do you notice about yourself when you're at your best?

_____

_____

_____

_____

_____

_____

What would the world be like without the involvement of healthy Type 4s?

_____

_____

_____

_____

_____

_____

 **VIRTUE**

Equanimity (Emotional Balance) is your virtue.

This allows you to have your feelings without allowing them to get in the way of your relationship with others.

What are some practical ways you can offer your virtue to others today?

Afterword

God's plan to restore the world involves all of us, which is why He made us so vastly different from each other in ways that reflect who He is.

That is why I'm so thrilled you picked up this book and have done the hard, but rewarding, work of looking into your heart. When you align with God's truth, you can support the kingdom, knit people together, and be the best *you* only you can be.

Growth is *not* easy. It requires us to surrender to God, depend on Him, and walk into His calling for us. But when we let go of our control and He takes over, He will satisfy our hearts, filling them with His goodness, and His blessings will flow into our lives and others' lives.

I can attest to God's transformative work having this ripple effect—reaching and positively impacting different parts of our lives and everyone we encounter. As I became more aligned with God's truth (and make no mistake, I'm still in progress!), the changes I was making helped transform my relationships with Jeff, my family, and other people around me. More and more friends, acquaintances, and even strangers were experiencing the transformation that comes from God through the tool of the Enneagram.

I can't wait to look back a year from now, five years from now, or even a decade from now, and hear about the ripple effects *your* transformation has created for hope, wholeness, and freedom. I'm excited about the path of discovery and growth ahead of you! What is God going to do in you with this new understanding of yourself and those around you? What are the things you'll hear Him whisper in your heart that will begin to set you free?

And how will your personal transformation bring positive change to the people in your life?

This is what I hope for you: First, that you will believe and trust in your identity in Christ. In Him, you are forgiven and set free. God delights in having you as His dear child and loves you unconditionally. This reality will radically change everything in you—it is the ultimate transformation from death to life.

Second, I hope that as you discover more about your Enneagram Type, you'll recognize how your personality apart from Christ is running *away* from your Core Fear, running *toward* your Core Desire, *stumbling* over your Core Weakness, and *desperate* to have your Core Longing met. As you become aware of these traits, you can make them the rumble strip alarms that point out what's going on in your heart. Then you can ask the Holy Spirit to help you navigate your inner world and refocus your efforts toward traveling the best path for your personality Type.

Third, I hope that God will reveal to you, both

in knowledge and experience, the transformative work of the Holy Spirit. With Him you can move toward growth, using all the tools of the Enneagram (the Levels of Alignment, the Wings, the Triads, the Enneagram Paths, etc.) to bring out the very best in you, the way God designed you to be. As a result, others will be blessed, God will be glorified, and you will experience the closeness of a Savior who will always meet your every longing and need.

May the love of Christ meet you where you are and pull you closer to God and others. And may you experience the joy of knowing His love for you in a deeper and more meaningful way.

Acknowledgments

My husband: I have to start by thanking my incredible husband, Jeff, who is my biggest cheerleader and supporter. He has helped me use the Enneagram from a biblical perspective and lovingly ensured that I expanded my gifts. Without his encouragement each step of the way, I never would have ventured into this world of writing. Thank you so much, Jeff.

My kids: Nathan and Libby McCord, you are a gift and blessing to me, and an inspiration for the work I do. Thank you for affirming me, being patient with me, and always believing in me. I pray this resource will bless you back as you journey through life.

ACKNOWLEDGMENTS

My family: To my incredible parents, Dr. Bruce and Dana Pfuetze, who have always loved me well and encouraged me to move past difficulties by relying on the Lord. To my dear brother and sister-in-law, Dr. Mark and Mollie Pfuetze, thank you for being a source of support.

My team at Your Enneagram Coach: You enable me to be the best I can be as a leader, and I'm so honored to be a part of our amazing team. Thank you for letting me serve, for showing up every day, and for helping those who want to become more like Christ by using the Enneagram from a biblical perspective. Thank you, Danielle Smith, Traci Lucky, Robert Lewis, Lindsey Castleman, Justin Barbour, and Monica Snyder.

My marketing team, Well Refined Co.: Thank you, Christy Knutson, Jane Butler, JoAnna Brown, and Madison Church.

My agent: Thank you, Bryan Norman, for helping me navigate through all the ins and outs so that this could be the very best work for our readers. Your advice was most beneficial.

My publisher: To Adria Haley and the team at HarperCollins Christian, thank you for allowing me to share my passion for the Enneagram with the world in such a beautiful way through this book collection.

My writing team at StrategicBookCoach.com: Thank you, Danielle Smith, Karen Anderson, and Sharilyn Grayson for helping me create my manuscript.

My friend and advisor: Writing a book is harder than I expected and more rewarding than I could have ever imagined. None of this would have been possible without my most-cherished friend and beloved advisor, Karen Anderson. I am thankful for her heart, her passion, and her help every step of the way. You beautifully take my concepts and make them sing. Thank you!

About the Author

Beth McCord has been using the Enneagram in ministry since 2002 and is a Certified Enneagram Coach. She is the founder and Lead Content Creator of Your Enneagram Coach and cowrote *Becoming Us: Using the Enneagram to Create a Thriving Gospel-Centered Marriage* with her husband, Jeff. Beth has been featured as an Enneagram expert in magazines and podcasts and frequently speaks at live events. She and Jeff have two grown children, Nate and Libby, and live in Franklin, Tennessee, with their blue-eyed Australian Shepherd, Sky.

Continue Your Personal Growth Journey *Just for Type 4!*

Get your Type's in-depth online coaching course that is customized with guide sheets and other helpful insights so you can continue uncovering your personal roadmap to fast-track your growth, overcome obstacles, and live a more fulfilling life with God, others, and yourself.